Photographer

Police officer (street)

Backhoe operator

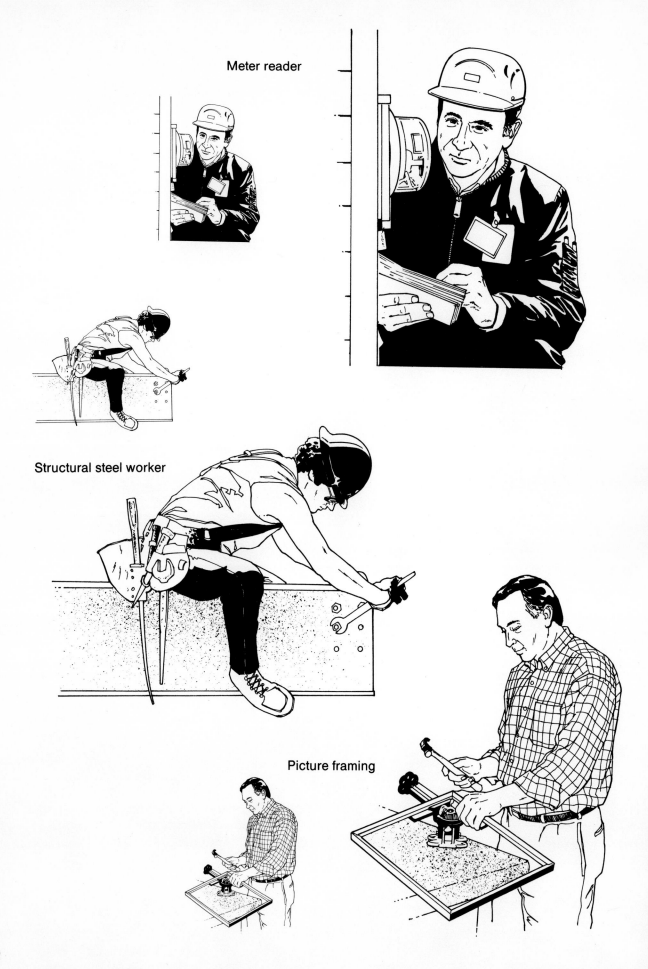

Meter reader

Structural steel worker

Picture framing

2

Fork lift operator

Surveyor

Auto mechanic

Police officer (traffic)

TV studio cameraman

Arc welder

Chef

Auctioneer

Oil rig workers

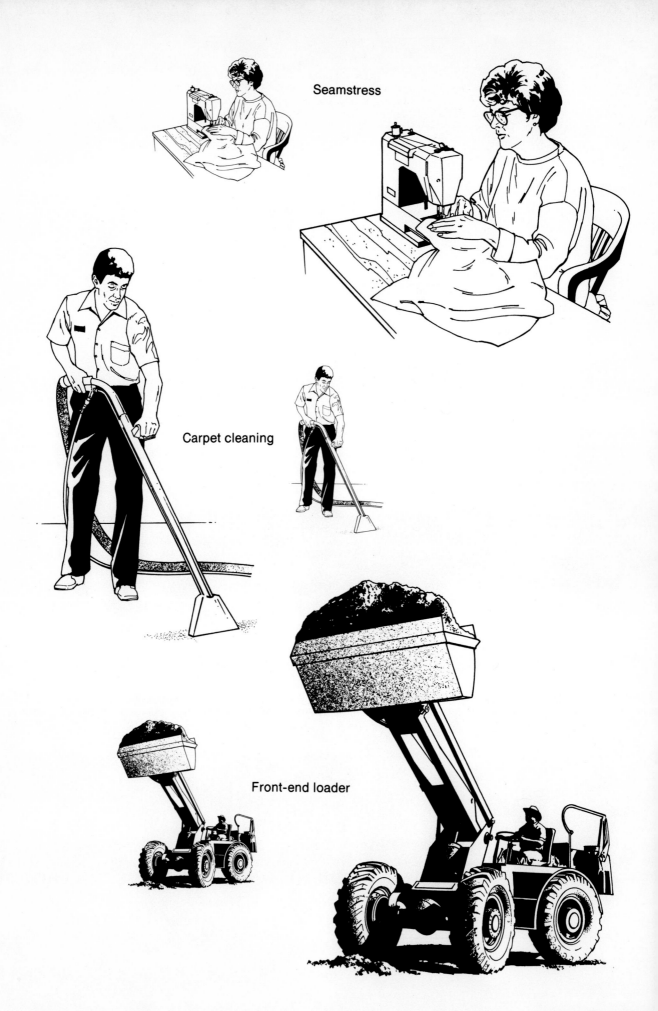

Seamstress

Carpet cleaning

Front-end loader

6

Dishwasher

Jackhammer operator

Bicycle repair

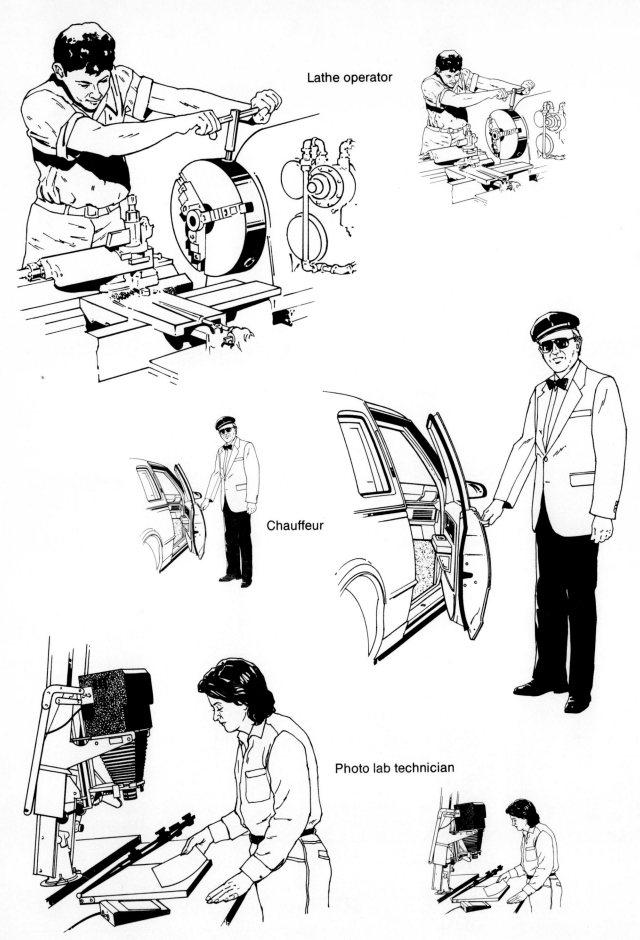

Lathe operator

Chauffeur

Photo lab technician

Construction engineers

Lumberjack

School bus driver

Railroad track maintenance

Police officer (highway patrol)

Chef

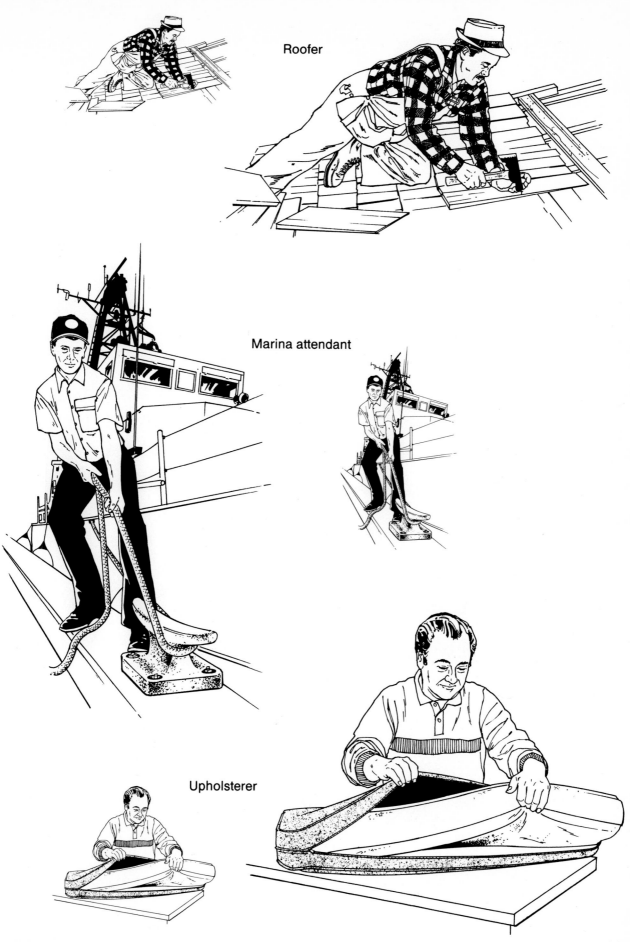

Roofer

Marina attendant

Upholsterer

11

Hazardous waste removal

Delicatessen

Sign painter

Air conditioner repair

Florist

Fisherman

13

Tobacconist

Landscaper

Electronics repair

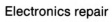

Aircraft maintenance

Bartender

Camera repair

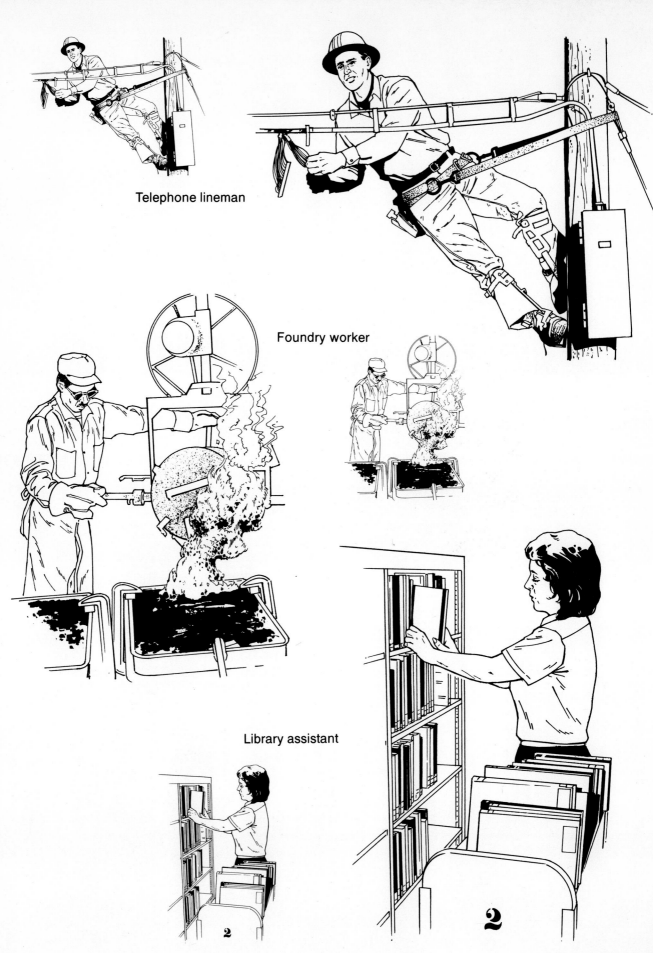

Telephone lineman

Foundry worker

Library assistant

2

2

Carpenter

Crossing guard

Electrician

17

Women's boutique salesperson

Bellhop

Telephone switchboard operator

18

Barber

Park ranger

Stonemason

Tree surgeon

Golf club maker

Zoo attendant

Cobbler

Cement finisher

Fence installer

Gas station attendant

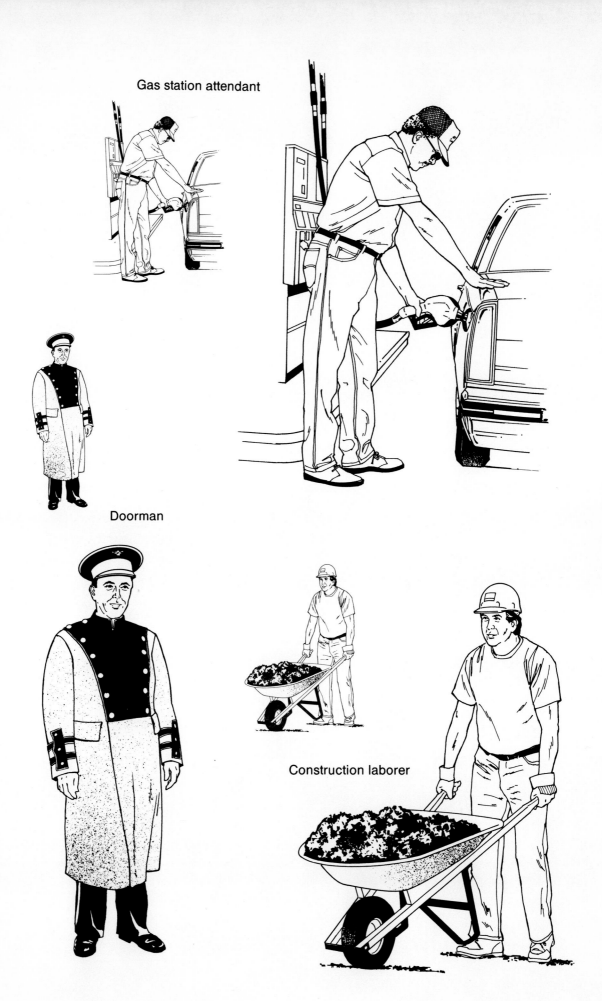

Doorman

Construction laborer

Hostess

Nursery

Window washer

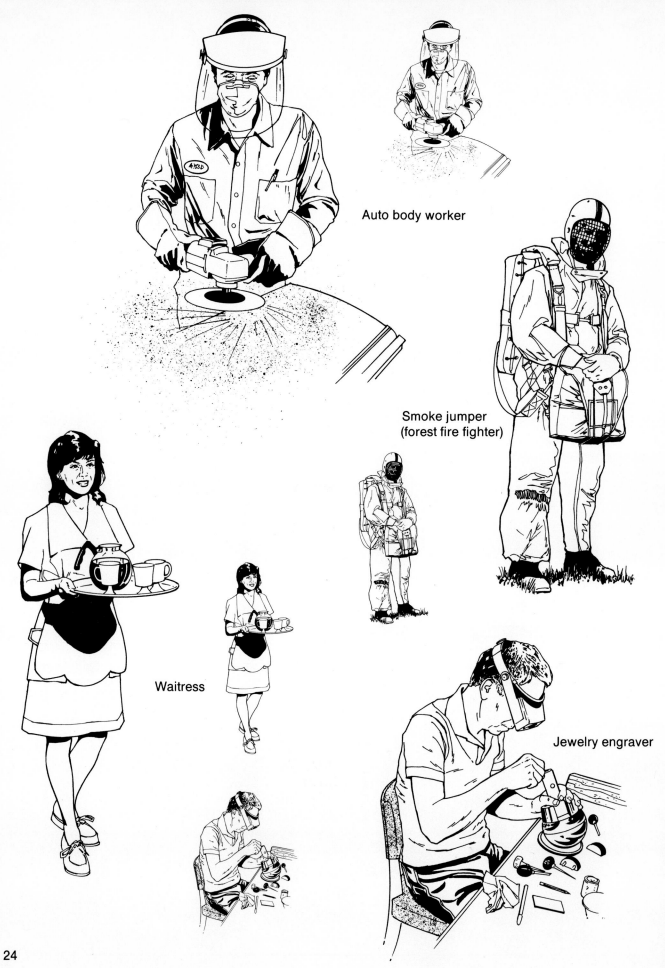

Auto body worker

Smoke jumper
(forest fire fighter)

Waitress

Jewelry engraver

Painter

Cocktail waitress

Heating installer

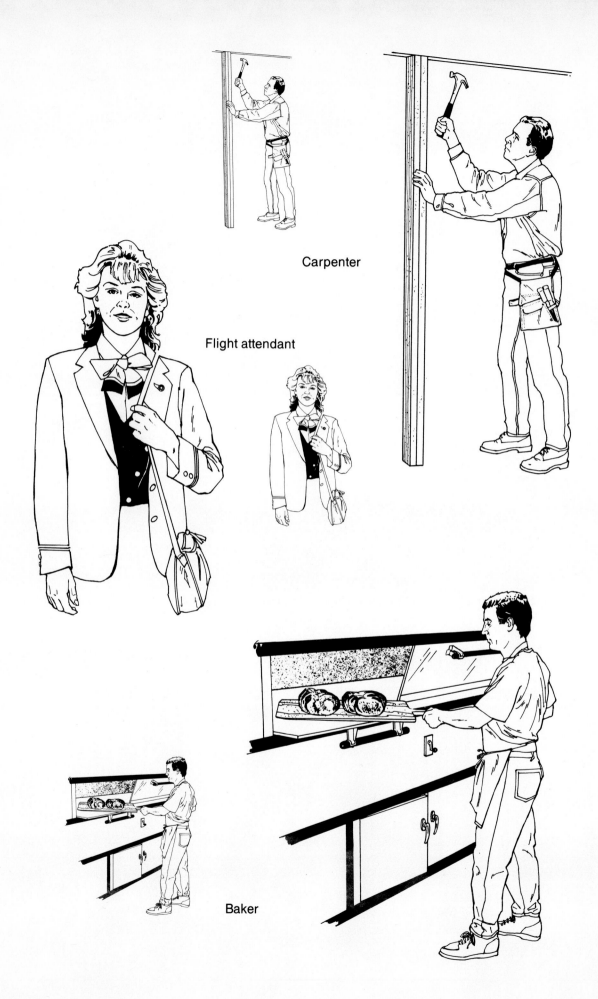

Carpenter

Flight attendant

Baker

Letter carrier

Garbage collector

Plumber

Bricklayer

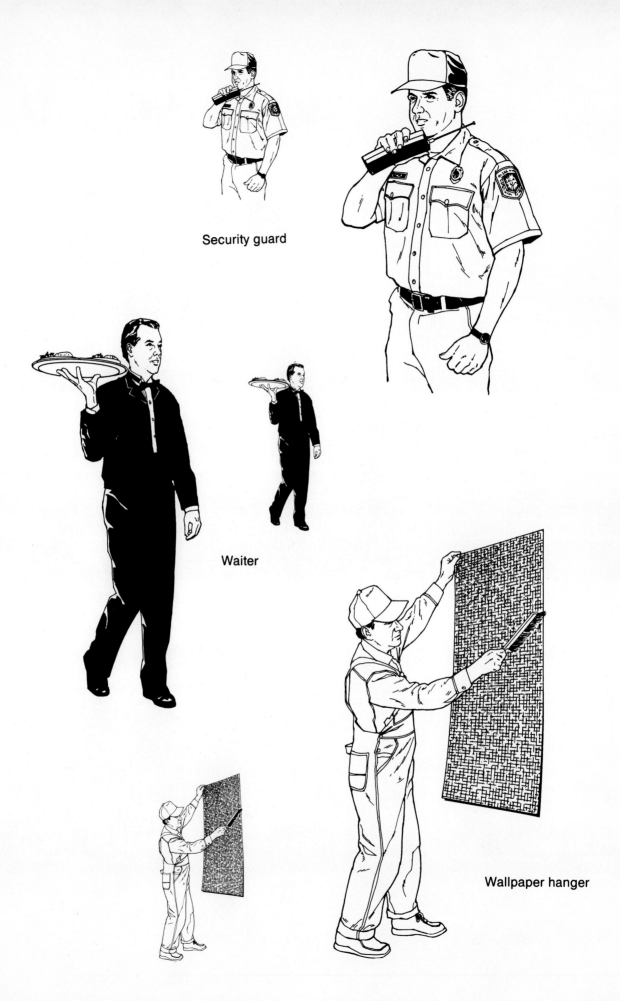

Security guard

Waiter

Wallpaper hanger

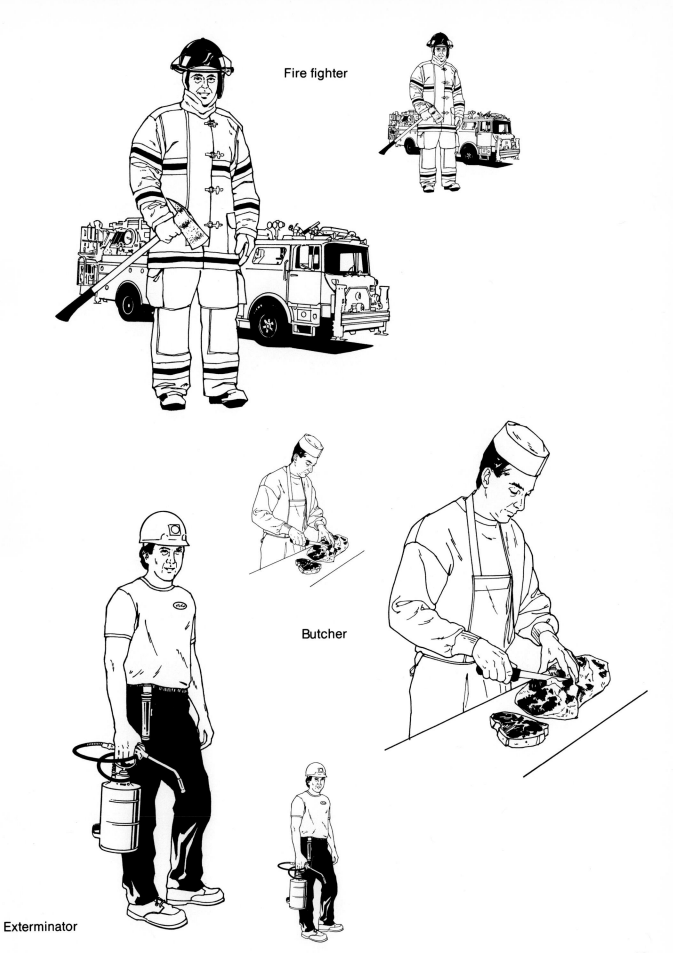

Fire fighter

Butcher

Exterminator

Librarian

Parcel service

Fire fighter

TV repair

Train conductor

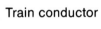

Farmer